Simple Rules
for Investing in
the Stock Market

The Simple But Powerful Long Term
Stock Investment Strategy That Works!

TRACEY EDWARDS

This is a Simple Rules Book
http://simplerulesbooks.com

Copyright © 2011 Tracey Edwards.

Cover design by Rodney Chapman

TABLE OF CONTENTS

INTRODUCTION

This book contains the stock picking strategy that I use to successfully make a profit in the stock market. It contains just five simple rules (and a few extra guidelines) that can be used by anyone to help them pick strong companies without having to know a lot about stocks to begin with.

I didn't set out to be an expert in the stock market and I'm still definitely not an expert, nor am I a financial planner or economist. In fact I'm just a regular person like you that one day, after being fed up with working a boring nine to five temp job decided to dabble in the stock market in an effort to try and make some money.

Of course becoming profitable and finding a winning strategy didn't happen immediately – it took a while before I was actually any good at the whole stock game. Over the course of five years I continued to work in crappy jobs while I read every book on the stock market I could and studied hundreds of different strategies. When I saved up my first thousand dollars I took the plunge and invested it into the stock market. It took another few years (and a few mistakes along the way) but eventually I had built up enough equity that I could leave full time employment and live on the proceeds of my investments.

My goal at the beginning was simply to build up a nice little portfolio and be able to support myself and while there have been both good and bad times when I have and haven't been able to do that (and we are in a rather bad time right now) overall I've been fairly successful with the methods I use. So by writing this book my hope is that it can help you to become successful as well and perhaps be able to build up your own successful little portfolio of stocks.

I think this book will appeal to those people who want to become more involved in buying stocks, so that they can gain more control over their finances, without having to learn too many complicated formula's and strategies.

It's not for everyone however. If you are already seriously involved in investing in the stock market then you may find my strategies rather simplistic. It's more for those everyday investors who are interested in learning more about what makes a good company and how to determine whether it would make a good investment.

Before I wrote this book, 5 Simple Rules for Investing in the Stock Market, I spent a lot of time reading other books in the market to see what was available. Most of the books I found were great on theory but not a lot of them had practical steps that you could take to choose your investments. So that's what I've done in this book. It doesn't contain much theory since you can already get that in many other wonderful stock market books but rather it contains practical 'how to' steps on what to look for. That's what I believe differentiates it from other books in the market.

I get quite specific in this book about what I look for. I know that I have strong opinions on what constitutes a good investment and it's likely that at times you may not agree with all of my rules.

If you have a different opinion – for example if you don't think debt to equity is as important as I do – then by all means just take out of this book those rules you do agree with and adapt them to your own experiences. These rules work for me, and while I know they can also work for others, you need to make investment decisions that are right for you and your situation. That goes for any financial decisions that you make. You need to be in control and do what is right for you.

The stock market can be very subjective. That's probably why there are so many different strategies and theories on which methods work. Even the experts can't agree sometimes. Some methods work, some of them don't. To be honest I think there are lots of different stock market investment strategies that can work, it just comes down to choosing a method that suits your style the best and sticking with it. But if you want to give my method a try, and I'm guessing that you do because you've purchased this book, then I'll tell you exactly what works for me. Of course in this day and age, you know that I can't guarantee that it will work for you. I sincerely hope it does of course, but alas I cannot guarantee it for fear of being sued. So use your own judgement.

If you're cool with that and you are keen to jump right in and see what these five simple rules are all about then by all means welcome aboard and thanks for buying the book.

The book is set out rather simply and flows in a logical style of how I choose the companies that I do.

- The first chapter talks about whether you should even consider investing in the stock market at all, especially in the rocky economic climate that we are in right now.
- Chapter two outlines the five basic stock picking rules that I use and why I narrowed it down to just five.
- The following chapters each cover one of the rules.
- Chapter three is about choosing the market leaders in the field. The blue-chip stocks if you will.
- Chapter four is what I consider to be the most important rule of all, and that is only choosing companies that have a Return on Equity figure of fifteen per cent or higher.
- Chapter five talks about the importance of the company having a positive earnings growth.

- Chapter six covers choosing companies that have low debt. You can potentially avoid many disasters by choosing companies that have not borrowed more than they can afford.
- Chapter seven looks back at the history of the stock price to see if it has a proven record of return for investors. While past performance is no guarantee of future performance it does tend to follow that if a company rises steadily each year that it will continue to do so.
- Chapter eight shows you how to determine whether the stock is trading at a fair price and how much you want to purchase it for.
- Chapter nine looks at investing for the dividend income. A sensible strategy for times when the market is rocky and you still want to make a good return from your investment.
- Chapter ten looks at the main reasons when you should sell your stocks and when to continue to hold.
- And finally I wrap things up in the conclusion.

Throughout each chapter I'll show which of the stocks from the Dow Jones Industrial Average make the rules and at the end we'll see which ones, if any, fit all of them and would be great companies to consider investing in.

So if you are ready, let's get started.

1

Should You Even Invest in the Stock Market?

"Too much of a good thing can be wonderful" – Mae West

About two or three years after I first started investing in the stock market my friend started making fun of me claiming that investing in stocks is no better than betting on horses. She argued that it was simply pure luck if you made any money and that I must be lucky to have not lost my money so far. She figured that 'gambling' on stocks was a fool's game and implied that I was a fool for even trying to learn it.

She had a point, because at that time I made as many mistakes as I did good decisions so while I was slightly ahead, I certainly wouldn't be considered a successful investor then. It wasn't until about the fourth of fifth year of investing in stocks (yes I'm stubborn to have lasted that long) that I really started to see a difference. And it was only after I stopped following many different complicated strategies (of my own devising) and simplified my approach that it all came together.

At first I started to wonder if my friend was correct and I was simply lucky. It's hard to believe that simplifying my investment techniques could pay off, especially since investing in the stock market is always made out to be so difficult. But while the process of choosing companies using my new method was simple, it was extremely powerful.

So I'm here to tell my friend that she was wrong (sorry babe). Investing is nothing like gambling on a horse race. For starters there doesn't have to be only one winner - I've already seen that more people than me are able to be successful in the market, so there is room for lots of people to make money at the same time. And secondly, who even said that it has to be a race? If you are investing for the long term then it makes no difference whether you jump now or in six months time. Invest when you are ready, both financially and mentally (yes it can be hard to put your money into the stock market – it can be scary – there is no rush).

And finally stocks are built on real businesses. Most companies really do want their business to succeed and make a profit – they are usually not fly by night operations (and if they are they wouldn't fit my five rules). It's not a gamble to want to invest in real companies and help them make a profit (and therefore see the stock price increase). It's just good business sense.

Of course right now you are probably saying to yourself "*that's all well and good Tracey, but all I hear is that people lose money in the stock market*". "*If you say it's so good then what's up with that?*"

Fair Question.

Especially given the current global financial crisis that we've just come out of where thousands of people lost a lot of money. I can certainly understand why people are hesitant about putting their money back into the stock market. You might be nervous about putting your faith in investing into companies and financial markets in case it all goes bust again taking your money with it. Especially when the other option is to keep that money in a nice safe bank account earning a decent interest rate.

Except for the fact that there is no such thing as a nice safe bank account with a decent interest rate anymore. Even the larger banks don't offer the high interest rates that they used to either. You are lucky if you find anything over 2% now. Keeping your money in a bank account – while might give you piece of mind – is not going to make you wealthy. In fact it could make you poorer as the rate of inflation overtakes the little interest that you may get.

So what are your other options? Property? – ok if you can afford it. Starting a business? – much riskier than the share market. Hoping that Grandma Betty leaves you her inheritance? – Let's just hope Granny invested in Microsoft back in the day then.

When it comes to wealth creation you don't have many options to get you started. And besides, is investing in the stock market really so bad? Could it be that if you have a proven and powerful plan for choosing great companies, a plan that will allow you to choose the best of the bunch, that it might be a good option for building wealth instead? Did those people that lost money have a good solid investment plan or did they leave their investments up to others and therefore didn't know what to do during a market crash and panic sold when they shouldn't have? Is it really possible that an everyday normal person can actually make money in the stock market if they know what they are doing?

Yes. Investing in the stock market CAN be really good for building wealth if you choose wisely.

And considering that the stock market has returned an average of 10% or more historically (even taking into account market crashes) then it's definitely something that you should consider if you want to build some real wealth.

This is actually a really good time to get back into the stock market. We've just been through a market crash so guess what is next in the cycle? Well if history is anything to go by then after every crash is the recovery. Are we about to enter another boom period? Who knows? I don't have a crystal ball to be able to say for certain, but I'm quietly optimistic. After every storm there is sunshine, so they say. But I can tell you that right now, everything is still quite cheap and moving up. Right now just might be a great time to think about investing back into the stock market. And once you have my rules down pat, you'll know which stocks make good investment sense and which ones to keep clear of. I hope you are excited.

Which Stock Market Does This Book Cover?

This book deals with the US stock market.

We live in a global economy today and we can invest anywhere in the world. While I started with the Australian stock market (because I live in Australia) I gradually moved to invest in a few different markets around the world adjusting my strategies as needed.

The American stock market is one of the biggest in the world, and it makes sense that I would eventually want to invest here since when I was learning all about investing in stocks I read every book I could get my hands on. The majority of them were books from American investors. Some of my favorite finance books included authors such as William J O'Neil, Stan Weinstein, Lawrence A Cunningham, Nicholas Darvas and Suze Orman.

Oh and let's not forget that my absolute hero is Warren Buffett (isn't every investors?) I read as much about his techniques as I could. What an inspiring man he is, whether you are an investor or not. Many of my rules are actually combinations of strategies I picked up from great investors including Warren Buffett and Nicholas Darvas combined with my own experiences as to what worked and what didn't. It's probably of no surprise to you then that the majority of the quotes in this book are attributed to Warren Buffett.

While my strategies can be used for any stock market around the world (I've already used them both in Australia and the U.S.), the rules listed in this book are primarily recommended for the American market, and in particular those stocks listed in the Dow Jones index and S&P 500 index. They represent the most well known and largest companies of all American stocks, and one of my first rules is to stick with the biggest companies so that you have more information and history to base your decision on.

This Book Is About Long Term Investing. Is That Better Than Short Term Investing?

There are quite a few different strategies for investing in the stock market but generally they fall into two main camps: long term investing (a term I consider at least two years – but mostly is around five to ten years or even longer) and short term investing (which could be as short as one day or as long as several months).

Most investors are usually in one of the two camps and say that their method is the best and that you couldn't possibly make the most money using anything else. You've probably heard it all before. *"Only invest in penny stocks", "Trading is losing money", "Long term investing is the only way to invest", "Come make $1K day trading".* Good grief, no wonder so many people are confused about investing.

Over the years I've tried a few different strategies and today I use both long and short term methods at different times and for different reasons. Since both methods can make you money I see no reason why I shouldn't use both of them. I actually don't think one is any better than the other; it's just a matter for what method you like using the best.

Of course the rules for both are quite different as you would expect them to be, which is why you need to know up front which set of rules you will be using for the particular company that you are interested in. You can't purchase shares in a company based on short term rules if you then decide that you are going to keep it if the stock price falls because you might just hold them for the long term now.

While you can, and should, use both long and short term strategies, you can't mix them up. If you buy for the long term, hold for the long term. If you buy for the short term, sell as soon as you either hit your profit or the price goes sour.

When I first started investing I was strictly a long term player. It was only as I got more confident about my investing techniques that I decided to venture into more short term methods as well. And then when the kids came along and I didn't have time to watch the market every day I reverted back to long term again.

Each method has its advantages and disadvantages. For example with long term investing you'll be doing most of your research up front and then when you buy, you'll be only checking in every so often to see what's happening - certainly no more than once or twice a year, to check that the company's fundamentals are still sound. However with short term investing its much more hands on and you'll be watching the stock price regularly, perhaps even daily, and adjusting your buy and sell price often.

Usually most people start out with long term investing first until they feel a little more confident in their investing skills. That's why I've decided to concentrate on just long term investing in this book, although I do plan to write another book using my short term rules in the future (yes I have some simple rules for short term investing as well – you would expect nothing less from me right?) But for now, let's get the basics down pat so we can get you confident and investment savvy using long term methods and start making some money.

How Much Money Do You Need To Get Started?

While I started with just $1,000, generally I tell people that you probably want at least three to five thousand dollars before you start to invest. If you haven't got that yet, then don't worry. A little saving will get you there in time. The market isn't going anywhere and even if you miss out on a really hot stock today there will be another around the corner soon anyway. Long term investment is about investing over many years – so whether you buy today or six months from now really shouldn't make much difference at all.

The reason I think starting with at least $3,000 is best is that you want to spread your risk by buying at least two to three companies to begin with. The best investors don't put all their money into one company and you shouldn't either. While you 'could' put a few hundred into a few different companies and still get away with starting with just one thousand dollars, usually the costs of brokerage and transactions will eat away at your profit making it not worth it. The objective here is to make as much money as you can, not to have it all whittled away on brokerage costs. And anyway most of the larger brokerage houses want you to deposit at least $2,000, sometimes more, to open an account with them before you even begin to think about investing it into a stock.

Speaking of which, you do have a broker don't you? There are lots of different online brokers to choose from, all charging different transaction costs to buy and sell shares so you'll need to have one ready to go if you want to invest in the stock market. Some of the top online brokers inside the U.S. include Wells Fargo, Firstrade, Fidelity, Vanguard, Schwab, E*Trade and more. If you are outside of the U.S. many online brokers in different countries handle U.S. trades so check if yours does and what the transaction costs are. Usually they are more expensive than trades within your own country, but often they are not too prohibitive.

Is Dollar Cost Averaging A Good Idea?

Dollar cost averaging is where you buy into the stock over an extended period of time, usually when you have the money available because you've just saved up some more and want to increase your holding.

I'm actually a big fan of dollar cost averaging because it means you can start with a small amount of capital and add to it when you have the funds. It has also shown to lower your risk slightly because you will be buying more stock at lower prices and less at higher prices.

Let's look at an example.

Say you want to buy $10,000 worth of XYZ Company, but right now you only have $2000. It's currently trading at $10.00 which means you could buy 200 shares.

Over the course of twelve months, each time you save up another $2,000 you invest it into the company again. So for example your trades might look something like this:

$200 \times \$10.00 = \$2,000$
$250 \times \$8.00 = \$2,000$
$285 \times \$7.00 = \$2,000$
$166 \times \$12.00 = \$2,000$
$154 \times \$13.00 = \$2,000$

At the end of the year you've now got 1055 stocks in the company. That's 55 more stocks than you would have had if you purchased all of them at the beginning of their year when it was trading at $10.00 (you could have bought 1000 stocks then). And since the price is now $13.00 your investment would be worth 1055 x $13.00 = $13,715, rather than 1000 x $13.00 = $13,000. That's an increased profit of $715 more.

Dollar cost averaging is a really good way of buying into the stock as you can afford it, and since you are buying more at lower prices and less at higher prices it actually can improve your profit with the same amount of money.

Should You Paper Trade First?

Paper trading is where you do all the research to find those great companies and 'pretend' to buy them. You write down which companies you would have purchased and keep track of them over time to see how well you could have done if you had invested in them in the first place.

Now there is nothing wrong with paper trading if that's what you want to do, however personally I have some issues with it.

Paper trading can work well with short term investing if you are testing out new strategies, but for long term investing, I don't know anyone who has the patience to sit back and wait a few years to see if their choices would have panned out. Even if you try and do it retrospectively (have a look at the financials of a company five years ago compared to today) you can't really say for sure if those are the companies that you would have invested in back then or not.

Besides most people act differently when real money is involved. When you are speculating you tend to be riskier in your choices and sometimes those risks pay off and sometimes they don't. When using your own money you tend to be more conservative and for long term investing conservative works much better.

Chapter

2

The Five Simple Rules for Long Term Investing

"Always invest for the long term." – Warren Buffett

When it comes to investing I could think of a dozen things I'd rather be doing that reading stock charts, turning on the Bloomberg channel or analyzing the current economic climate. Now don't get me wrong, I'm interested in investing and I'm really good at it (well I think so anyway), but I just don't want to spend hours doing it. So I had to come up with a plan that would allow me to find great investment opportunities quickly but was still powerful enough to work well. I wanted big results from little effort.

I'm a true believer in the concept of keeping things simple. Many people think I'm making things too simplistic and often dismiss the power of my rules, but I don't care. I'm making money using them. And many others that I've shared my rules with are too. And isn't that what's important? I believe that you shouldn't be tied to your investments, but they should work for you. They should quietly and happily be increasing in value while you keep a lazy eye on them to make sure all is good.

Of course you'll need to know a few little things like how to read a financial statement and what a company's Return on Equity (ROE) is because it's important to know whether it's a good company or not. Knowing which companies are good investments and which are bad gives you financial control. You want to have control yourself about what you pick and not leave it up to anyone else to choose for you. I have seen far too many 'experts' lately who have taken people's money and squandered it unnecessarily. I don't want that to happen to you. That's why you need to become a little bit savvy about what you invest in. And that's why I think you'll find my rules for long term investing give you that knowledge to choose winners in the market.

Besides many economists don't do as well as your regular stay at home investor so knowing more isn't a prerequisite to earning more in the market. By all means listen to them if you want to learn more – I love hearing their advice and reasons why markets move like they do, I find it fascinating (yes I'm weird like that) – all I'm saying is that a little knowledge can be all you need. Why complicate matters when what you are doing works so well?

While my rules may be simple enough to use, they are far from simple in the companies they choose. In fact by using the combination of the five rules together you will be able to separate the good from the bad in most cases. And that is extremely powerful. I didn't make up these rules from thin air either – I studied some of the most successful investors on the planet and adapted their strategies and what they look for in choosing great companies to my own investing needs.

Nearly every successful investor looks at companies with high Return on Equity, considers earnings growth as a good indicator of a strong company, and examines the amount of debt a company holds before they invest their money with them. I'm just simplifying the process for you. Allowing you to become a savvy investor and share in the successes that I've had by investing in the stock market.

So here are the five rules that I use to find great companies to invest in:

1. Only choosing companies that are listed in the Dow Jones or S&P 500;
2. Choosing companies which have a Return on Equity (ROE) of 15% or higher;
3. They should have positive earnings growth;
4. Low debt; and
5. A history of good returns for investors.

See I told you they were simple.

Once you combine all the rules that I've put together, you can see that you really are only choosing companies that have good financials and have already proven themselves to be winners in the past. That means you will be able to avoid all the smaller and lesser known companies that are more risky. I'm not saying that you can't make money with these smaller companies, but you have to agree that there is far more risk with them than there is with the bigger, more stable companies. I'm also not saying that by choosing these larger companies that you'll make less money. In fact some of the larger companies such as Microsoft, Disney and Cisco have gone on to make fortunes for investors as you no doubt already know.

Call me boring, but I like nice safe, stable, strong companies that are likely to weather the good and bad times in the market (and make me a small fortune in the process).

Throughout the book I'll be using examples from the Dow Jones Industrial Average index (DJI). I've chosen to use the companies with the Dow Jones throughout this book since the index contains the biggest thirty companies in terms of market capitalization in the U.S. I'll be using these mainly for way of example of explaining the concepts for you, but also because I don't have the room to list all of the five hundred companies in the S&P 500 here (*that'd make the book huge*). But feel free to do the research on the top 500 companies yourself so that you get a much larger pool of good companies to choose from. You don't want to limit yourself to just a handful otherwise you might miss out on some really good investments.

So let's get stuck right into the good stuff and look at each rule in a little more detail so that you know exactly what you need to look for.

3

Rule 1: Choosing the Market Leaders

"Never invest in a business you cannot understand." – Warren Buffet

In life we tend to follow the leaders to see what their opinions are and perhaps follow their advice in hopes of making our lives better and inspiring us to be better versions of ourselves. Businesses are no different. In every industry some companies just do things better than others. These companies are considered the market leaders in their field and the ones that we will be looking at in the first rule.

It makes sense that choosing the best of the best is a good investment decision but it wasn't always the case for me. When I first started investing I'd choose companies at random simply because someone gave me a stock tip and told me that the price as about to explode. Nine times out of ten that didn't happen and I would lose money on these smaller 'hot' stocks.

My aha moment came when I took a serious look at what the big investment managers who run the mutual funds were choosing. In nearly all cases they included stocks from the biggest companies in their selections and they seemed to be doing really well.

So I did a little experiment and for six months only chose companies that were considered the market leaders to see if they would do better than other previous companies that I had been investing in. While they generally moved less than other companies (their stock prices didn't jump around so much) and you didn't get the huge rises (or dramatic falls) these companies just seemed to plod along on their own improving month to month in a nice stable fashion.

So I made it my first rule.

It made things easier straight away because it's overwhelming trying to narrow down your selection and choose a company to invest in. There are hundreds, if not thousands, of different companies that you could choose to buy shares in.

In the U.S. around 8,500 companies trade on the New York Stock Exchange (the world's largest exchange), in Australia there are over 2,000 companies listed on the ASX, and the London Stock Exchange in the U.K. has over 2,500 companies listed. Also companies are being added and withdrawn regularly so it can be difficult to keep up with them all.

Therefore this rule means that you only look at no more than the top 500 (or even less in some instances). In the U.S. that means looking at only those companies listed in the S&P500 or smaller index.

And if you are feeling incredibly lazy like I sometimes am, then you can even narrow down your selection further to only the top 200 or even the top 100. There have been times where I've only looked at the top 50 too. Of course if you don't find a winner in the top 50 companies, then it's probably time to look a little wider – but if you do it can save a lot of time.

The companies listed in these indices represent the largest companies in terms of market capitalization listed on the stock exchange. They are the market leaders. Bigger companies tend to hang around a lot longer (they don't crash and burn like smaller unknown companies tend to do frequently) and while they still can get into trouble (anyone heard of Enron?) they are much less likely to than smaller companies. That's why I am more confident on choosing from the better known stocks rather than a company I have never heard of before.

Another reason why sticking with the larger companies is important is because there is usually a lot more financial information available about them, and if you want to make an informed decision then it's a good idea to get as much information as is available on that company. You can find out what the company does, how much profit it makes, how long it has been listed on the exchange, and what the return to stockholders has been in the past. This historical data is crucial to helping you select a company that fits the simple investing rules.

You probably already know some of the larger companies listed on the stock exchange anyway, or at least have heard of them. Here is a list of the top 30 market leaders that currently makeup the Dow Jones Industrial Average index that we'll be using as examples throughout this book (how many of the thirty have you heard about?)

You can skip this part if you already know about them, but if you at all curious as to which companies actually do make up the DJI then here they are:

AA – Alcoa makes aluminum products for both consumers and industry for use in aircraft, automobiles, packaging, defense and building and construction.

AXP – American Express is best known for their credit and charge cards as well as their travel related services worldwide including travellers checks.

BA – The Boeing Company designs and manufactures jetliners, spacecraft and even military missile defense although most consumers know them best for their commercial jet aircraft.

BAC – Bank of America is one of the largest and well known banks in the U.S. providing financial services to individuals, businesses and corporations.

CAT – Caterpillar make machinery for the construction and farming industry. You might have seen a Caterpillar crane when you pass a building site or a tractor when you drive by a farm field.

CSCO – Cisco is in the technology industry and designs and sells information technology products worldwide including routers, IP networks, servers and more.

CVX – Chevron is in the oil and gas industry and markets its products under the names Chevron, Texaco and Caltex. They both mine and develop crude oil and natural gas and refine their products into petroleum products.

DD – EI du Pont de Nemours is a science and technology company that operate in many different segments from Agriculture & Nutrition, Electronics & Communications, Safety & Protection to Pharmaceuticals.

DIS –Walt Disney is an entertainment company that ranges from television networks, radio, film and movies, and of course the iconic parks and resorts.

GE – General Electric operates under a number of sectors starting from its energy infrastructure right though to technology, media and financial services.

HD – Home Depot stores are best known for selling a wide range of home improvement and building materials. They also offer handyman and installation services for those that would prefer others to do it for them.

HPQ – Hewlett Packard is a technology company which make personal computers, calculators, printers, and more recently financial leasing services to consumers.

IBM – IBM provides information technology products worldwide from infrastructure to computers. They also produce software systems for business such as WebSphere and Tivoli software.

INTC – Intel design and sell computer chips and circuits for the computer and communications industry worldwide. Their microprocessor products are used in most new computers, notebooks, servers and handhelds.

JNJ – Johnson & Johnson is a healthcare company that makes products ranging from baby care, skincare, and oral care to medicinal and healthcare products.

JPM – JP Morgan Chase is a financial holding company that is best known for its investment banking services although they also do retail banking, commercial banking and asset management.

KFT – Kraft Foods is one of the world's largest manufacturers of consumer goods under various brand names including Kraft, Oscar Mayer, Philadelphia, Maxwell House, Jacobs, Oreo, Cadbury and more.

KO – Coca-Cola makes carbonated beverages and syrups for the world. I'm sure you've consumed a Coca-cola beverage in your time (I know I have!)

MCD – McDonalds owns and franchises its range of McDonald's restaurants around the world. I'm sure you've heard of them. Big Mac anyone?

MMM – 3M is a diversified technology company that is involved in a whole range of different products from consumer and office supplies, to health care products, industrial and transportation and communications.

MRK – Merck & Company produce prescription medicines and vaccines to consumers and the medical field including both human and animal health care products.

MSFT – Microsoft develops and manufactures computer software programs and devices from Windows operating systems to Xbox 360 gaming consoles.

PFE – Pfizer researches and produces pharmaceutical products for the health care market and also consumer products including dietary supplements, cold remedies and infant formula.

PG – Proctor & Gamble make a wide range of consumer goods many of which you use every day including Crest, Gillette, Olay, Pantene, Old Spice, Bounty, Cascade, Pringles and more.

T – AT&T is a telecommunications company that offer networking, telephone and internet services. They also publish the yellow and white pages directories and offer advertising in them.

TRV- The Travelers Companies have a range of financial products with an emphasis on insurance for consumers, businesses and corporations. Their biggest (and most well known) product is auto insurance.

UTX – United Technologies produces a wide range of products from heating and air conditioning to aerospace systems, elevators & escalators, aircraft engines and even fire and security systems.

VZ – Verizon is one of the largest deliverers of communication services including broadband, wireless and wired services to consumers, businesses and governments.

WMT – Wal-Mart is a large discount department store with both online and offline (physical) stores. They stock and sell just about anything you could want to buy (currently they have over one million products available online).

XOM – Exxon Mobil includes the brands Exxon, Exxon Mobil, Mobil and Esso and is involved in chemicals, lubricants and fuels for the consumer, aviation and marine industry.

I always find it interesting to know what the company does before I invest in it. After all, stocks are more than just a little letter code – they actually do something, have people working for them and exist in the real world.

As I've mentioned I'll be using examples from these market leaders throughout this book, simply because they are so well known, but don't be afraid to look outside this list to other companies listed in the S&P 500 when you are looking for companies yourself to choose from.

So there. The first rule was easy and didn't really take up much of your time at all. Just that you have decided to choose from the market leaders only. Whether that's as small as the Dow Jones or as large as the S&P 500 comes down to how much research you want to do.

I told you these rules were simple.

4

Rule 2: Return on Equity Must Be 15% or Higher

"Focus on return on equity, not earnings per share." – Warren Buffett

If you ask any investor what they consider to be one of the most important factors as to whether a company is a great investment and they'll probably tell you to look for a high Return on Equity (ROE). In fact most stock market investors consider that Return on Equity is one of **the most important figures to determine how well, financially, that the company is doing**.

In investment terms Return on Equity is a measurement of how much profit the company makes from the money that shareholders have invested into it. You could work it out yourself by dividing the shareholder's equity from the company's net income. But of course you don't need to as most companies prominently display the ROE figure in their financial figures. Warren Buffett also thinks it's pretty important and so if it's good enough for the big man, it's definitely good enough for us.

So, the second rule for choosing a great company to invest in for the long term using my simple rules is that the Return on Equity (ROE) must be 15% or higher.

I first started using the figure of 15% or more after Buffett said in an interview in 1972 that a ROE of <u>at least</u> 14% was desirable and he rarely invests in companies that fall below this figure. All of the companies that Berkshire Hathaway invests in have higher than average ROE's including stocks such as Coca Cola, American Express and Gillette whose average return on equity figures are generally above 20% and sometimes as high as 40%.

If we look back over history it's clear to see that a company that has a good return on equity does seem to fare much better in the stock market than those companies that have low or negative ROE's.

Finding the ROE figure is generally pretty easy and is usually listed on the Key Statistics page when you are researching a company. Here is the ROE of Exxon Mobil Corp (XOM) showing its Return on Equity as 23.43%.

(image overleaf)

Exxon Mobil Corp. (XOM)

More On XOM

QUOTES

Summary

Order Book

Options

Historical Prices

CHARTS

Interactive

Basic Chart

Basic Tech. Analysis

NEWS & INFO

Headlines

Financial Blogs

Company Events

Message Boards

Market Pulse NEW!

COMPANY

Profile

▶ Key Statistics

SEC Filings

Competitors

Industry

Components

ANALYST COVERAGE

Analyst Opinion

Key Statistics

Data provided by Capital IQ, except where noted.

Valuation Measures	
Market Cap (intraday)[5]:	412.80B
Enterprise Value (Mar 29, 2011)[3]:	410.72B
Trailing P/E (ttm, intraday):	13.38
Forward P/E (fye Dec 31, 2012)[1]:	9.98
PEG Ratio (5 yr expected)[1]:	1.01
Price/Sales (ttm):	1.21
Price/Book (mrq):	2.83
Enterprise Value/Revenue (ttm)[3]:	1.20
Enterprise Value/EBITDA (ttm)[3]:	7.35

Financial Highlights	
Fiscal Year	
Fiscal Year Ends:	Dec 31
Most Recent Quarter (mrq):	Dec 31, 2010
Profitability	
Profit Margin (ttm):	8.89%
Operating Margin (ttm):	12.01%
Management Effectiveness	
Return on Assets (ttm):	9.60%
Return on Equity (ttm):	23.43%

Figure 4.1 – Table showing the Return on Equity for Exxon Mobil Corp as 23.43%. Image screenshot from finance.yahoo.com

The figure is recalculated every time the company releases its latest financial figures (whether that is quarterly, every 6 months or yearly depending on how often the company reports) so you will need to recheck every so often to make sure that if you invest in a company that still has over 15% ROE as you continue holding it.

In case you are wondering, the (ttm) after the Return on Equity stands for trailing twelve months and means that it is the current figure for the past year based on the last reporting period. This means the figure is much more up to date than it would be if they only used, say the December end reporting period every year.

I've done some of the homework already for you, and here are the ROE figures for the thirty companies listed in the Dow Jones Industrial Average as at April 2011:

(image overleaf)

Company	ROE
AA	2.45%
AXP	26.49%
BA	130.18%
BAC	-0.97%
CAT	26.74%
CSCO	17.38%
CVX	19.29%
DD	35.09%
DIS	12.36%
GE	10.55%
HD	17.44%
HPQ	21.85%
IBM	64.59%
INTC	25.16%
JNJ	24.89%
JPM	10.17%
KFT	8.06%
KO	41.86%
MCD	34.51%
MMM	28.40%
MRK	1.66%
MSFT	44.35%
PFE	9.29%
PG	16.74%
T	18.14%
TRV	12.16%
UTX	21.40%
VZ	11.95%
WMT	22.03%
XOM	23.43%

Figure 4.2 - Spreadsheet showing the ROE of the 30 companies within the DJI. I've highlighted those with ROE's over 15% for you.

As you can see, out of the thirty companies, twenty of them have ROE's over 15%. Some of them, like Boeing (BA) are quite a bit over 15% with its ROE being 130.18%. While that's a good sign, you shouldn't necessarily just choose the company with the highest ROE. As long as it's over 15% then you know the company is doing ok and fits the first rule.

If you were only looking at these 30 companies, you can now move twenty of them onto your next rule – that they have good earnings growth figures. However, if you are looking at the companies within the S&P500 then it might take you a little longer to get the figures, but you'll have a much bigger pool of good companies to choose from.

5

Rule 3: Companies Should Show Positive Earnings Growth

"An investor should ordinarily hold a small piece of an outstanding business with the same tenacity that an owner would exhibit if he owned all of that business." – Warren Buffet

A good indication that the company is doing well is that they consistency grow their earnings year after year. And I like consistency. In fact while I like being surprised with expensive gifts (hint hint), that isn't the case when it comes to choosing companies to invest in. Give me a boring and stable company that is shows good growth in its earnings and I'm a happy girl.

Many investors like to look at earnings growth when evaluating a company to invest in because it can correlate to a steady increase in stock prices over time as well. I've seen many investors say that looking for 'double-digit' earnings growth (anything that is above 10%) is important because that means the company is doing really well, but I personally think anything positive is good no matter how small. Generally larger companies don't have as high an accelerated growth as new companies do so it's important to examine all the factors.

When looking for a company's earnings growth, it's usually expressed as Quarterly Earnings Growth (yoy) in the companies key statistics which means it compares the growth in earnings over the past three months compared to that in the same quarter the previous year. The higher the number (expressed as a percentage) the better the company is doing compared to the previous year.

Now while it doesn't measure the share price return of the company directly (very often when earnings results come out the stock price decreases for a short time), over the long term and if all its other fundamentals are good, you can usually be confident that it should increase in value in the future.

After return on equity, a positive earnings growth percentage is one of the most important determinates for choosing great companies to invest in.

So How Do You Find The Earnings Growth Of A Company?

Just like the ROE, the Earnings Growth is listed on the Key Statistics page of the company along with the rest of most of its financials. You can see in this figure that the Qtrly Earnings Growth for EI DuPont de Nemours is 26.70%.

El DuPont de Nemours & Co. (DD)

More On DD

QUOTES
Summary
Order Book
Options
Historical Prices

CHARTS
Interactive
Basic Chart
Basic Tech. Analysis

NEWS & INFO
Headlines
Financial Blogs
Company Events
Message Boards
Market Pulse NEW!

COMPANY
Profile
▶ Key Statistics
SEC Filings
Competitors
Industry
Components

Key Statistics

Data provided by Capital IQ, except where noted.

Financial Highlights	
Fiscal Year	
Fiscal Year Ends:	Dec 31
Most Recent Quarter (mrq):	Mar 31, 2011
Profitability	
Profit Margin (ttm):	9.88%
Operating Margin (ttm):	12.32%
Management Effectiveness	
Return on Assets (ttm):	6.45%
Return on Equity (ttm):	34.10%
Income Statement	
Revenue (ttm):	33.72B
Revenue Per Share (ttm):	36.91
Qtrly Revenue Growth (yoy):	15.80%
Gross Profit (ttm):	8.36B
EBITDA (ttm):	5.53B
Net Income Avl to Common (ttm):	3.32B
Diluted EPS (ttm):	3.58
Qtrly Earnings Growth (yoy):	26.70%

Figure 5.1 – Table showing the Quarterly Earnings Growth for EI DuPont as 26.70%. Image screenshot from finance.yahoo.com

Again, this figure is recalculated every time the company releases its latest financial figures.

To help you out, here are the Qrtly Earnings figures for the thirty companies listed in the Dow Jones Industrial Average as at May 2011:

Company	Qrtly Earn
AA	n/a
AXP	33.00%
BA	12.90%
BAC	-35.60%
CAT	317.20%
CSCO	-17.90%
CVX	36.40%
DD	26.70%
DIS	54.30%
GE	76.50%
HD	n/a
HPQ	15.80%
IBM	10.10%
INTC	39.40%
JNJ	-23.20%
JPM	67.00%
KFT	n/a
KO	274.00%
MCD	2.10%
MMM	-0.70%
MRK	0.00%
MSFT	30.60%
PFE	276.80%
PG	11.10%
T	-60.80%
TRV	29.70%
UTX	16.90%
VZ	224.80%
WMT	27.30%
XOM	69.00%

Figure 5.2 - Spreadsheet showing the Quarterly Earnings Growth of the 30 companies within the DJI.

The quarterly earnings growth for some companies can be huge, such as Caterpillar (CAT) with growth of 317.20% and for others it has decreased, such as AT&T (T) with -60.80%. As I've mentioned, I really only want to know it's increasing year to year, so as long as it's positive I'm happy.

If you take the twenty companies from Rule 1 that had good ROE figures, we can now look at their earnings specifically to see if they all still fit the rules:

Compa ▾	ROE ▾	Qrtly E: ▾
AXP	26.49%	33.00%
BA	130.18%	12.90%
CAT	26.74%	317.20%
CSCO	17.38%	-17.90%
CVX	19.29%	36.40%
DD	35.09%	26.70%
HD	17.44%	n/a
HPQ	21.85%	15.80%
IBM	64.59%	10.10%
INTC	25.16%	39.40%
JNJ	24.89%	-23.20%
KO	41.86%	274.00%
MCD	34.51%	2.10%
MMM	28.40%	-0.70%
MSFT	44.35%	30.60%
PG	16.74%	11.10%
T	18.14%	-60.80%
UTX	21.40%	16.90%
WMT	22.03%	27.30%
XOM	23.43%	69.00%

Figure 5.3 - Spreadsheet showing both the ROE & Quarterly Earnings Growth of the 30 companies within the DJI. I've highlighted those that fit both rules so far.

Applying our rules it looks as if a few more companies have dropped out because they didn't have positive earnings growth figures. I've also not included Home Depot (HD) because it has earnings growth listed as N/A. Often companies will do this for various reasons including a period with zero growth, negative, or non-disclosed earnings. Whatever the reason, if it's not listed it can't be included in the rules and so it's out.

That leaves us with fifteen companies that are still contenders. So the next rule is to make sure that they don't have high debt. Let's find out which ones do and are therefore out and which ones are still showing promise.

6

Rule 4: Choose Companies with Low Debt

"The ability to say "no" is a tremendous advantage for an investor." –
Warren Buffett

The fourth rule when it comes to investing in the stock market over the long term is that you should always try and choose companies that have a low amount of debt. The reasons for this are probably pretty clear – you want to make sure that any company that you are thinking of investing in isn't about to get into trouble if the economy gets shaky again. You need to know that the company that you choose will be able to survive a downturn in the market and having too much debt can make them more vulnerable. Not to mention you could have easily avoided disasters like Enron just by looking at its debt to equity figure.

Even in good economic conditions, if a company has a lot of debt it means that any changes to the current interest rates will affect them financially. If the interest rate goes up, then so does their expenses.

It's the same as if you borrow money to buy a house that might be a little above what you can afford to pay. At first everything is rosy and you have the home of your dreams but rising interest rates will soon mean that you have to eat Ramen noodles to make the interest payments. Added to that is that life often throws a curve-ball or two to keep you on your toes – you might get pregnant, or move jobs, or even marry The Bachelor who wants you to move to Los Angeles to further his television career. Anything can happen!

I'm not saying that you should avoid companies with debt altogether, in fact some companies should have high borrowings because it helps their business grow and thrive, but if it's too high then I might be less inclined to add that company to my 'buy' list.

So what is too high? Generally for me I don't like the debt to equity ratio to be anything more than 75%. Keeping it below 75% means that even if the company does go belly up that they'll still have some money left over to pay out their debts, and that sometimes includes shareholders too.

Different types of companies usually have different levels of debt to equity ratios depending on the type of business that they do. Companies that are involved in property could have quite high levels of debt due to the many property loans that they hold, or at the other end of the table some companies like banks have no debt equity ratios since they are the ones that actually lend the money not borrow it. This is why for lending institutes such as Bank of America (BAC) it will show N/A for Debt/Equity which is perfectly fine.

Interestingly, there is a strong correlation with high debt and high earnings growth, because the company has usually borrowed to fund a new project or business venture causing a spike in earnings.

Here are the debt / equity ratios for all the stocks within the Dow Jones Industrial Average for their most recent quarters (mrq).

Compa ▾	Debt/E ▾
AA	50.50
AXP	376.47
BA	291.71
BAC	n/a
CAT	251.15
CSCO	33.36
CVX	10.85
DD	108.62
DIS	32.10
GE	370.99
HD	51.81
HPQ	49.27
IBM	132.82
INTC	4.66
JNJ	29.65
JPM	n/a
KFT	80.01
KO	75.08
MCD	78.62
MMM	34.70
MRK	31.49
MSFT	24.63
PFE	49.89
PG	46.60
T	59.10
TRV	26.19
UTX	44.73
VZ	68.87
WMT	69.61
XOM	9.83

Figure 6.1 - Spreadsheet showing the Quarterly Earnings Growth of the 30 companies within the DJI as at May 2011. I've highlighted those companies that have debt equity ratio's lower than 75%

The companies that have debt to equity ratios below 75% are highlighted in the spreadsheet. As you can see, about two thirds of them have acceptable ratios that fit the rule. Don't forget to include those companies that have no debt to equity ratios (the banks) as well in your good to go list.

When doing your research, you'll notice that there are some very high debt to equity ratio's, such as Boeing Airlines (BA) in this example. Boeing obviously carries large loans for its fleet of aircraft (last I checked, airplanes were expensive). That could be a good thing for the company, they wouldn't be in business without having something to fly their passengers around in, but it still doesn't fit my rule so I wouldn't go ahead with this company at this stage. Sorry Boeing it's nothing personal, but rules are rules.

Yes, it does mean I'll be missing out on some great companies (if you check out Boeing's chart you can see that they are doing very well and I potentially could have missed out on investing into it). However it just is one of those rules that I like to stick with because I get nervous with companies that have too much debt. Don't worry there are plenty of other great options for those companies that do fit my rules.

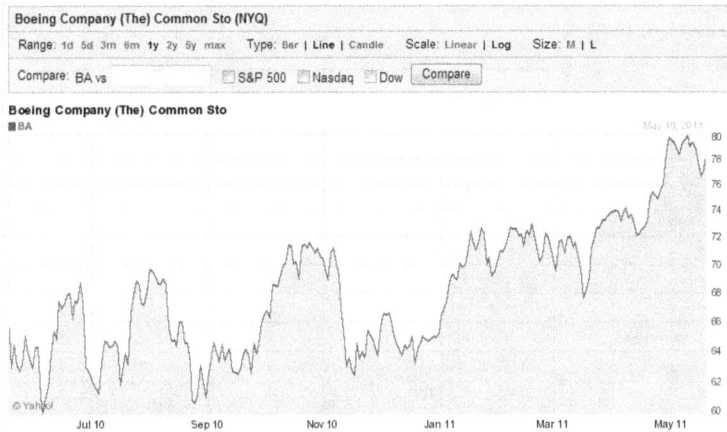

Figure 6.2 – *Boeing's Company (BA) chart for the past 12 months. It started at below 66 and has reached 78 at May 19, 2011. Image screenshot from finance.yahoo.com*

Where to find the Debt to Equity Ratio

Finding the Debt to Equity ratio for a company is relatively easy and can be found by looking at the company's key statistics page. It should be listed under the Balance Sheet section. Here you can see Boeing's Debt to Equity ratio for its most recent quarter (mrq) as 291.71. Again, that could change by the time the company posts its most recent financials.

Boeing Co. (BA)

More On BA

QUOTES
Summary
Order Book
Options
Historical Prices

CHARTS
Interactive
Basic Chart
Basic Tech. Analysis

NEWS & INFO
Headlines
Financial Blogs
Company Events
Profile
▶ Key Statistics
SEC Filings
Competitors
Industry
Components

ANALYST COVERAGE
Analyst Opinion
Analyst Estimates
Research Reports
Star Analysts

Key Statistics

Financial Highlights	
Income Statement	
Revenue (ttm):	64.00B
Revenue Per Share (ttm):	86.47
Qtrly Revenue Growth (yoy):	-2.00%
Gross Profit (ttm):	12.46B
EBITDA (ttm):	6.22B
Net Income Avl to Common (ttm):	3.38B
Diluted EPS (ttm):	4.53
Qtrly Earnings Growth (yoy):	12.90%
Balance Sheet	
Total Cash (mrq):	7.77B
Total Cash Per Share (mrq):	10.53
Total Debt (mrq):	11.69B
Total Debt/Equity (mrq):	291.71
Current Ratio (mrq):	1.16
Book Value Per Share (mrq):	5.30
Cash Flow Statement	
Operating Cash Flow (ttm):	2.28B
Levered Free Cash Flow (ttm):	-2.29B

View Financials
Income Statement - Balance Sheet - Cash Flow

Figure 6.3 - *Boeing Company's (BA) Key statistics showing its Debt/Equity ratio as 291.71. Image screenshot from finance.yahoo.com*

So how is our list of the companies within the DJI going so far? Well from our list of fifteen remaining contenders, we can see that seven of them had debt to equity ratios that were too high and didn't fit the rules. That leaves us with just eight companies that still are in the running.

Compa ▼	ROE ▼	Qrtly Ea ▼	Debt/Ec ▼
AXP	26.49%	33.00%	376.47
BA	130.18%	12.90%	291.71
CAT	26.74%	317.20%	251.15
CVX	19.29%	36.40%	10.85
DD	35.09%	26.70%	108.62
HPQ	21.85%	15.80%	49.27
IBM	64.59%	10.10%	132.82
INTC	25.16%	39.40%	4.66
KO	41.86%	274.00%	75.08
MCD	34.51%	2.10%	78.62
MSFT	44.35%	30.60%	24.63
PG	16.74%	11.10%	46.60
UTX	21.40%	16.90%	44.73
WMT	22.03%	27.30%	69.61
XOM	23.43%	69.00%	9.83

Figure 6.4 - *Spreadsheet showing ROE, Quarterly Earnings Growth and Debt to Equity of the 15 of the 30 companies within the DJI.*

Well we are nearly there! Just one more rule before we put it all together to determine if there are any winners that we might want to invest in. Next up we look at how the company has performed over the past few years by looking at the share price history.

7

Rule 5: Share Price History has shown a Good Profit

"Do not take yearly results too seriously. Instead, focus on four or five-year averages." – Warren Buffett

My last rule of long term investing requires two main factors and they are:

1. The company should have been publicly listed for at least five years or more (so that you can have more confidence that this isn't a flyby night operation), and

2. Over those past five years they have shown that they can return a decent profit for shareholders.

This isn't an easy task, especially considering the turbulent three or four years that we have just been through, but even in bad economic times some companies do much better than others. Those are the ones that you want to seek out and invest in. Those are the ones that are likely to be winners and make you wealthy.

I would have to say, that out of all my rules so far this is one that I do give a bit of lee-way with. It used to be that I only looked for companies that increased by at least 15% p.a. average over the last five years, and while this is relatively easy to find when the market is bullish and all good companies are rising in price over the long term. When the market turns bearish, as it's likely to do every now and then, then sometimes no matter how good the company is doing the stock price will decrease anyway simply due to market pressure.

However I didn't want to discount this rule either, since I consider what a company has done in the past a very good indication of what it will do in the future, so I just amended it a bit. I still require that it has done well in the past but I am more lenient that it doesn't have to have returned as much as 15% p.a. on average every year over the last five years. I'm certainly not going to discount a company because it only returned an average of 8% per year. That is still much higher than I can get in any high interest savings account so still represents a good return on investment.

Has The Company Been Publicly Listed For At Least Five Years or More?

The first question you need to determine is has the company been listed for at least five years?

It's actually pretty easy to find out if a company has been publicly trading for at least five years, just by looking at its chart. If it has five years of trading history then it's been around long enough for us to consider it. You don't have to look at any fancy charts or determine if the price is going up or down yet. (Charting is more for short term investing which is another strategy all together). All you need to do is look and see that it does in fact have five years of data. That's enough for us.

You can look at your company's chart by typing its company code into your own online brokerage site or a free finance site like finance.yahoo.com. Let's have a quick look at The Travelers Companies, Inc. (TRV) chart which you can find by choosing Basic Chart.

Yes, one glance and you can see that it's been trading for five years. Done. Analysis over. Ahh I love simplicity.

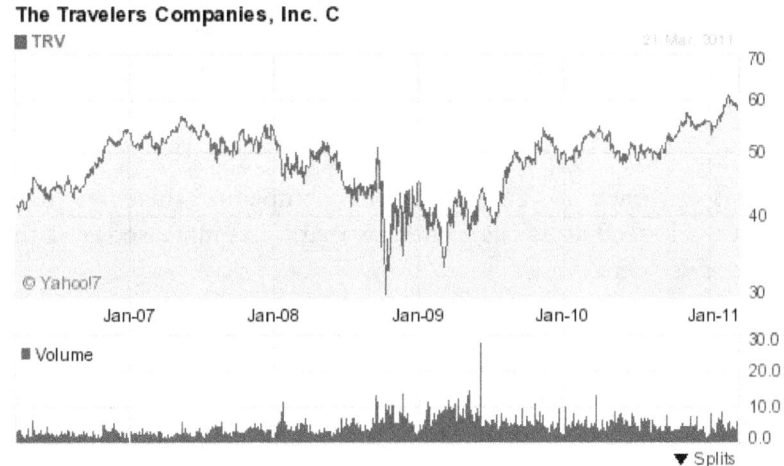

Figure 7.1 – *Simple 5 year stock price chart for The Travelers Companies (TRV) showing it has in fact been trading for at least five years. Image screenshot from au.finance.yahoo.com*

Now that was pretty easy (told you). The next part of the rule however is a little more difficult to find out because we need to have a look at what the average p.a. of that company was over the past five years and that takes a little detective work. But don't panic it's still pretty easy to find out – and many brokerage houses will even give the information to you from their website. But for the rest of us, here is how to work it out.

What is the Average Stock Price Return over the Past 5 Years?

Now you could just find out the stock price of the company from five years ago and compare it to the stock price today (and that would be a perfectly legitimate analysis according to this rule), but I like to get a little more information so I can see how consistent it has been. This is especially useful if I'm trying to decide between a handful of stocks and up until now haven't had a clear winner. Just choosing the one that has made the most money in the past might sound like a good idea (and it might be ok), but I just feel better having the little extra bit of information.

Let's go back to The Travelers Companies since we have already looked at its chart and saw that it has increased over the past five years.

Most research houses will allow you to see the historical prices of a stock in a few different ways. On Yahoo Finance it's in the left hand menu bar under (of course) 'Historical Prices'. You can set a date range of the prices that you want to find out about and get back the information as daily, weekly or monthly prices. You can also find out just want the dividends was if you were investing for income only.

Let's look at the simpler way first and determine what the stock price was five years ago and what it is now to compare the two.

Five years ago on March 21, 2006 TRV closed at $41.47.

At the time of writing (on March 21, 2011) it closed at $58.95.

Just looking at those figures, we can see that in the past five years the stock price increased by $17.48 representing an increase of 42% which (simplistically) averaged over five years is 8.4% p.a. To find out the average just divide the total increase by the number of years you are looking at, so in this case it's 42% divided by 5 (years) to equal 8.4%.

In this case TRV would fit this rule just perfectly. Sure it isn't the lovely 15% p.a. that I would have liked, but it still is a very decent result given the tumultuous few years that we've just been through.

But what if you want a little more information and want to know year in year out what it did. Well that's easy too and should only take you a few more minutes to work out. You already have today's price and the price five years ago, so it's just a matter of getting the prices of the years in between and then working out the increase or decrease per year.

TRV Stock Prices over the Past 5 Years

Date	Closing Price	Increase / Decrease from Previous Year
March 21, 2006	41.47	-
March 21, 2007	52.66	27%
March 20, 2008	47.79	-9%
March 20, 2009	38.81	-19%
March 22, 2010	53.39	38%
March 21, 2011	58.95	10%
	Average p.a.	9%

As you can see with TRV, the stock price has been very volatile jumping from highs of rising 38% in one year to lows of losing 19% in the previous year. Overall it still has a positive result over a five year period though which is what we are looking for. Remember we are investing in this for the long term, and over the long term this company has increased in stock price.

Whether you just use the simplified version of taking the price five years ago compared to today, or would prefer to see what the company did year on year is a up to you. Both methods are perfectly fine and will give you similar results (give or take a few percentage points), it's just that I like to use the second method so I can see how the company has done year to year. Just having that extra bit of information makes me feel a little more in control and better informed about the decision to buy into the company or not. By all means, choose whichever method that you prefer though.

Using the simpler method, now let's look at the stock price returns over the past five years for all the companies in the Dow Jones. In this table, I've included the stock prices from 20 May 2011 compared to five years prior on 20 May 2006.

Compa	5 yrs ago	Today	Profit/L	PL / 5
AA	31.98	16.67	-47.9%	-9.6%
AXP	52.23	51.82	-0.8%	-0.2%
BA	84.61	78.02	-7.8%	-1.6%
BAC	48.27	11.69	-75.8%	-15.2%
CAT	72.78	105.30	44.7%	8.9%
CSCO	20.87	16.66	-20.2%	-4.0%
CVX	58.47	103.87	77.6%	15.5%
DD	42.81	53.43	24.8%	5.0%
DIS	30.15	41.38	37.2%	7.4%
GE	34.16	19.96	-41.6%	-8.3%
HD	38.94	37.39	-4.0%	-0.8%
HPQ	32.02	36.13	12.8%	2.6%
IBM	80.28	170.59	112.5%	22.5%
INTC	18.36	23.54	28.2%	5.6%
JNJ	59.90	66.39	10.8%	2.2%
JPM	42.75	44.00	2.9%	0.6%
KFT	31.49	34.99	11.1%	2.2%
KO	43.65	68.46	56.8%	11.4%
MCD	34.15	82.51	141.6%	28.3%
MMM	84.31	94.71	12.3%	2.5%
MRK	27.90	37.38	34.0%	6.8%
MSFT	20.51	24.72	20.5%	4.1%
PFE	23.82	21.03	-11.7%	-2.3%
PG	54.15	67.46	24.6%	4.9%
T	25.28	31.40	24.2%	4.8%
TRV	44.65	62.81	40.7%	8.1%
UTX	62.70	88.10	40.5%	8.1%
VZ	30.90	37.32	20.8%	4.2%
WMT	47.32	55.48	17.2%	3.4%
XOM	60.45	82.33	36.2%	7.2%

Figure 7.2 - Spreadsheet showing the increase or decrease in % of all the stocks in the DJI. I've highlighted those that have made a positive return over the past 5 years in the profit/loss column, and only highlighted those companies that have returned at least 5% p.a. in the PL/5 column.

You may realize that we've been through the GFC during this time and many of the stocks have not yet fully recovered. But there are still some companies that have done well over the past five years.

The profit/loss column has any results highlighted that are positive and the second column has been divided by 5 to adjust for an annual rate (simplified version). I've only highlighted in green those results that have averaged at least 5% p.a. over the past five years. I've chosen five percent because this seems to be higher than most high interest savings accounts right now are offering and you want your investment to do better than a basic savings account (otherwise what would be the point in investing in the stock market in the first place if you could do better elsewhere?)

And as you can see eleven of the thirty companies in the Dow Jones have returned a positive result. But what about our list so far of the contenders from the DJI that have up until now fit all of our rules. How did they fare over the past five years? Well let's have a look shall we?

At the end of the last rule we still had eight companies out of the thirty that were still in the running. They were Chevron (CVX), Hewlett-Packard (HPQ), Intel (INTC), Microsoft (MSFT), Procter & Gamble (PG), United Technologies (UTX), Wal-Mart (WMT) and Exxon Mobil (XOM).

If we look at their returns over the past 5 years you'll see that from the spreadsheet listed above in figure 7.2 that they returned the following:

Compa ▼	5 yrs ag(▼	Today ▼	Profit/L ▼	PL / 5 ▼
CVX	58.47	103.87	77.6%	15.5%
HPQ	32.02	36.13	12.8%	2.6%
INTC	18.36	23.54	28.2%	5.6%
MSFT	20.51	24.72	20.5%	4.1%
PG	54.15	67.46	24.6%	4.9%
UTX	62.70	88.10	40.5%	8.1%
WMT	47.32	55.48	17.2%	3.4%
XOM	60.45	82.33	36.2%	7.2%

Figure 7.3- Spreadsheet showing the average share price return for some of the companies listed in the Dow Index.

Only four have returned an average share price return of 5% or higher. And only one of those, Chevron, has increased by an awesome average of 15.5% over the past five years. A very nice return for investors indeed!

While I still wouldn't discount the other ones that returned less than this, it's definitely a promising sign that these four stocks fit all of our simple rules.

So it's time to go ahead and buy them now right?

Er, not so fast. While it would be perfectly ok to go ahead and buy into these great companies since they have proven that they have excellent fundamentals, are nice and stable and have a history of good share price return for investors there are still a few more factors to take into consideration. And first we need to look at the current stock price to see if it represents good value for investors or not.

8

Buying Those Great Stocks – But At What Price?

"You are neither right nor wrong because the crowd disagrees with you. You are right because your data and reasoning are right." – Warren Buffet

By now you should have a great list of companies that you trust and want to invest in and you are ready to fork out your hard earned cash and become a stock holder in the company. Awesome. But are you really going to purchase them at any old price? No. Not if you want a good deal first.

You want to make sure that the companies that you want to buy are not overpriced first. One of the secrets that Warren Buffett says that he looks for is to find a great company that is currently underpriced in the market. The theory being that pretty soon everyone else will realize its true value as well and the price will increase (making you some lovely profits). So I've created another rule (well more like a guideline really) about when to buy and at what price.

And I also let you know about when to sell too (that's coming soon). But before we look at whether we should go ahead and buy right now, let's go back over what we've learned so far and examine the companies in the Dow Jones that we have been looking at.

Our first rule was that we only look at companies in the S&P 500. Ok, so we only used those in the Dow Jones for the examples here for brevity sake, so yes they all fit this rule.

The next rule was that they had ROE's of at least 15%. Twenty of them did, so they stayed in.

Next was that they had positive earnings growth. Most of them did as well with a few exceptions. We lost the following companies from our list because they had negative earnings growth for the latest quarter results: Cisco, Johnson & Johnson, the 3M Company, and AT&T. That still left us with 16.

The next rule was that they had debt levels below about 75%. And here we lost a few more companies from our list including American Express, Boeing, Caterpillar, EI du Pont de Nemours, IBM, Coca-Cola, and McDonalds.

Finally we wanted to make sure that the companies had a good record of return over the past five years. And from our results of those that returned at least 5% p.a. over the past five years, from the remaining companies still within our rules, these four companies made it through: Chevron (CVX), Intel (INTC), United Technologies (UTX) and Exxon Mobil (XOM).

These 5 simple rules have combined together to allow us to focus on only those great companies with strong fundamentals and a proven track record. In a nutshell we are able to find some real potential winners that could possibly go on to increase in value and price in the future. So now it's time to look at when (and if) to buy them.

The Price You Should Pay for a Great Company

You've probably realized by now that prices of stocks increase and decrease quite regularly and while some companies are more stable than others generally over the course of a week the price can vary quite a lot. One day it's up and the next it's down. These daily fluctuations can actually work in your favor when you want to buy into a stock because you don't have to purchase at the current market price and can set a price at a level that will allow you to get a good deal.

Although it can be naïve to try and buy at the lowest price and sell at the highest (not even the professionals can do that), it doesn't mean you have to settle for the current price if it is too expensive.

So my strategy for determining the buy price for a stock is simply to multiply the earnings per share (EPS) price by sixteen. After a bit of experimentation, I've found that companies that are currently trading at or below sixteen times EPS (as long as all the other rules are in place) provide the best value for your money.

EPS stands for Earnings per Share and represents how much of the company's earnings are allocated to shareholders. It can be represented as basic or diluted; with diluted meaning that it takes into account any unexercised stock options on the stock.

It's pretty simple to find the EPS figure because, yep you guessed it, it's already listed for us on the company's key statistics page. In the image below you can see that Disney's EPS is currently 2.27. 16 times 2.27 is 36.32, so the price you would pay for Disney would be no more than $36.32 per share. And since today it's trading at $38.01 *(June 16, 2011)* it's slightly overpriced and therefore doesn't represent good value right now.

Walt Disney Co. (DIS)

More On DIS	Key Statistics	
QUOTES		
Summary	**Financial Highlights**	
Order Book	**Fiscal Year**	
Options	Fiscal Year Ends:	Oct 2
Historical Prices Profile	Most Recent Quarter (mrq):	Jan 1, 2011
▶ Key Statistics	**Profitability**	
SEC Filings	Profit Margin (ttm):	11.32%
Competitors	Operating Margin (ttm):	18.58%
Industry	**Management Effectiveness**	
Components	Return on Assets (ttm):	6.46%
ANALYST COVERAGE	Return on Equity (ttm):	12.36%
Analyst Opinion	**Income Statement**	
Analyst Estimates	Revenue (ttm):	39.04B
Research Reports	Revenue Per Share (ttm):	20.32
Star Analysts	Qtrly Revenue Growth (yoy):	10.00%
OWNERSHIP	Gross Profit (ttm):	6.73B
Major Holders	EBITDA (ttm):	8.99B
Insider Transactions	Net Income Avl to Common (ttm):	4.42B
Insider Roster	Diluted EPS (ttm):	2.27

Figure 8.1 – *Walt Disney's (DIS) Earnings per Share (EPS). Image screenshot from finance.yahoo.com*

Let's have a look at the four companies that we have found that fit all of our rules and see if they are currently trading at a price that is at or below 16 x EPS.

Company	EPS	16 x EPS	Current Price at 16 June 2011	Trading at/below 16 x EPS?
Chevron (CVX)	10.30	164.80	99.43	YES
Intel (INTC)	2.01	32.16	21.42	YES
United Technologies (UTX)	4.74	75.84	84.35	NO
Exxon Mobil (XOM)	7.02	112.32	79.22	YES

Three of the companies within the Dow Jones Industrial Average fit all the rules AND they are currently trading at less than sixteen times EPS which means they represent great value. They would be the companies that I'd go ahead and place on my 'buy now' list.

But what would happen if we didn't find any companies that were trading at a good price?

How Set In Stone Is This Rule?

It always happens. Just when you've found an awesome company to invest in, it's trading higher than you want to pay. Should you go ahead and invest anyway? Hmm depends.

Now is probably a good time to have a look at the history of the stock price over the past six or twelve months to see if it's likely to come down. Since the stock market has ups and downs you can often use this to your advantage, especially if you have a jumpy share that likes to rise and dip regularly.

In the case of Disney, we saw earlier that it was currently trading above 16 x EPS, but over the past year has recorded prices from as high as 44.34 and as low as 30.72. If you are patient, two things may happen. One is that it might dip down low enough for you to want to buy it, or two when the next quarterly report comes out, the EPS figure might increase meaning that it will once again fit into the 16 x EPS rule because it will be worth more.

If it does neither of these things but you still think it's a good long term investment then it's time you made a judgement call. There have been times when I've purchased slightly above 16 x EPS and it was a brilliant decision, and other times when I wished I'd waited because a few weeks later it dipped down to a good price. Generally I hold off though, especially when I have a list of other companies that are trading at a fair price that I could purchase instead.

What If There IS More Than One Company That Fits The Rules, Should I Buy All Of Them?

That depends on how much money that you have to invest in the stock market. If you can afford it then sure! Go ahead and diversify your portfolio and buy all of them so that you minimize your risk. Of course that's fine if you have only a handful of good companies, but it gets a bit tricky if you find more than ten or so that fit all the rules (and if you are working with the whole S&P 500 then it's very likely).

Generally, depending on your budget of course, it's good to put at least $3,000 - $5,000 per company when you are starting out. Obviously if you only have $10,000 to invest that limits you to two or three different stocks. If you have more then you can allocate more per company.

But If You Find That There Are Twenty or So Good Companies Should You Buy All of Them?

I personally don't like to hold more than ten or so companies at a time. But that's because I don't want to keep track of more. But holding more is fine if you can keep track of them all. That's what the big mutual funds do anyway (hold a big bundle of companies to diversify and lower their risk).

Obviously the more companies that you have in your portfolio the lower your risk is going to be because you are not putting all your eggs in to the one basket (company) so it's a fine balance between how many you want to hold and keep track of, and how risky you want to be. But personally I like holding no more than ten companies only. Ten is a good balance between diversifying your portfolio enough to lower your risk but not enough to dilute any returns that you might make.

Besides the more companies you have to choose from the easier your decision becomes because you can choose the best of the bunch. Of course you can always choose which ones to buy based on how much dividends that they pay which brings us to the next chapter.

9

Investing for the Dividend Income

"Wild swings in share prices have more to do with the "lemming- like" behavior of institutional investors than with the aggregate returns of the company they own." – Warren Buffett

So now that you've found some great companies to invest in that have an excellent chance of increasing in value over the long term, can it get any better?

Yes it can.

Because many of these companies also pay high dividend yields, making them an excellent source of income as well as capital growth. In fact many investors who don't like the volatility of the stock market will often invest just for the dividend income they produce since many companies pay yields much higher than a regular savings account. Since it's hard push today to find a high interest savings account that pays an interest rate of more than two percent per annum within the United States, companies that offer upwards of three percent dividend yields (and sometimes as high as five or six percent) can look very attractive.

Most of the time the companies that pay the highest yields are those whose businesses receive income payments themselves such as property investment companies, insurance companies and so on. That's why they can afford to pay out such high dividends to investors because they receive high fees from customers themselves. Of course any company can pay high dividends; it isn't limited to only those service businesses.

Not all companies pay dividends however. It's up to the Board of Directors to decide whether to pay out a portion of the profits to investors or use that money to grow the business. This is why many investors believe that you can only invest for the income OR the growth (whereas I believe you can have both).

Investing in companies for the income also lowers your risk, because even if the company or market as a whole experiences volatility usually the dividend yield remains fairly stable. So receiving a regular check every quarter can mitigate the risks involved in investing your money in stocks. Sure your initial investment isn't secure like it is in a regular bank account, but the higher yield can usually compensate for that. Let's look at an example.

Comparing Savings Account Interest vs. Dividend Yield

Let's imagine that you were an income investor and were only interested in the dividend yield. Let's also say that you have $10,000 to invest.

If you put it into a standard savings account earning 1.5% (fairly average) over a five year period you'd earn around $778 in interest. You would still of course keep your initial investment of $10,000 as well since that money is secure.

Let's instead say that you invested in Verizon (one of the high dividend yield companies within the Dow Jones) who pays an average of 5.4% yield.

Five years ago on September 18, 2006 Verizon was trading at $37.10. Buying $10,000 worth of Verizon would have meant you purchased 269 shares. 269 x $37.10 = $9,979.90.

As of writing, Verizon is now trading at $36.72 which means that your initial investment is now worth $9,804.24 (269 x $36.72). This represents a loss of $175.66.

However, each year Verizon paid out dividends remember? So over that period, you would have also received checks totalling well over $2,000 for the five year period.

Sure your initial investment is slightly down, but the amount of money that you would have made in dividend income has more than covered that and is nearly triple what you could have earned in a regular savings account. That's why investing for the dividend income is so attractive to many people. It doesn't matter as much if the stock market is rocky because each quarter you still receive your dividend check in the mail.

You can check out the dividend yields on the Key Statistics page, the same page where we are getting all of our other financial figures. It's listed under Dividends and Splits and you can also see here when the next payout is. Generally though, payments are usually January, April, July and October.

Investing for income sounds great, and it is, but you also know that I like to choose companies with strong fundamentals that have the potential for high growth. Most investors think that you can't invest for both growth and income, however I disagree. I think that you can find great companies and then see if they pay a good dividend yield as well, so that you can have the best of both worlds.

The Companies from the Dow Jones That Fit All the Rules AND Have High Dividends

So far in this book, we narrowed down the selections to the following three companies who fit all of the five simple rules and were trading at below sixteen times earnings. Let's now look at what their dividend yields are.

Chevron – 3.1%

Intel – 3.8%

Exxon Mobil – 2.5%

I consider anything above three percent a good dividend yield (and anything above five percent outstanding), so of these companies both Chevron and Intel look like the best bets.

Why it's Not Just Retiree's that Invest for the Dividend Income

It makes sense that those people that want a regular investment income such as retiree's, will choose to invest for income rather than growth since they don't usually have time on their side to wait until the market increases, they need the money now to live on. But the same can be said for anyone that wants to receive a regular income; college students, single parents, anyone really. Of course you do need a fairly substantial capital to earn a full time living simply from the investment checks.

To receive a yearly income of $50,000 you'll need to have invested a cool one million dollars first. (You DO have one million just sitting around waiting to invest in stocks don't you? No?) This is the reason why generally it is only retiree's that can afford this strategy, but even if you have a few thousand you still should be taking advantage of the dividend yields since it lowers the volatility of your investment. It's been proven that those that invest in companies that pay good dividend yields make higher returns overall than those that don't.

But that doesn't mean you should simply find the stock paying the highest dividend yield and be done with it.

Currently Frontier Communications (FTR) has a dividend yield of 10.7% (extremely high). Five years ago, it was trading at $13.66 and today it is trading at $7.11. That represents a loss of around 48%. Now over time you would have received dividends of course, but even the high yield that this company pays out wouldn't have protected you. On an investment of $10,000 your initial investment would now be worth $5,200 and over that time you would have received around $4,000 in dividend income. While it sounds nice, the high dividend payout wouldn't have been enough to protect your initial investment from eroding. That's why it's still important to choose strong companies first and THEN look at the dividend yield so that you have an increased chance of making a profit.

If you can find great companies that are paying good dividend yields then you'll be able to ride out the volatility and still make money.

Should You Take The Cash Or Re-Invest Your Dividends?

Some companies that pay out dividends may give you the option to re-invest the dividend amount back into the company in the form or more stocks. This is usually done at a slight discount to the current market price to make it more attractive to stockholders. But is it a good idea to do this, or should you take the cash instead?

Both are fine options, and it really comes down to preference over whether you need the money or not in the short term. If you rely on the dividend income, or even just think it's a nice bonus then by all means take the cash, but if you already have an income and the odd dividend check isn't going to make a whole lot of difference to your bottom line then reinvesting your dividends back into the company is a very good idea.

Now you still will be taxed on those dividends whether you receive them as cash or reinvest, since they are still classed as income, so don't think that just because you don't get the check you are off the hook in this regard. Speak to your accountant for the best tax advice.

The main benefit of re-investing your dividends back into the company is that you can take advantage of the magic of compound interest. The more stock that you hold, the more dividend income that you make, so by re-investing that dividend amount and buying more stock, the next time you get a bigger piece of the pie. Over a long period of time you can essentially be holding more than double the amount of stock that you started with, each time getting 'paid' the dividend back in the form of more stock.

Dividend reinvestment plans work best on growth stocks or those companies that pay a high yield since both can accelerate the value of your portfolio.

10

When to sell your stocks (if at all)?

"Much success can be attributed to inactivity. Most investors cannot resist the temptation to constantly buy and sell." – Warren Buffett

If you've purchased a company according to the long term investing rules, it's a safe bet that you want to hold it for a long time. And that means anything from five to ten years (or even longer in some cases). However there will be occasions when you want to sell, so it's time to look at some of the reasons why you might want to sell your stock and either cash in for a profit or jump ship if the price starts to fall.

If you've purchased for the long haul then it's important not to watch the stock reports every night. It can make even the most Zen investor start to break out into a cold sweat every time the price decreases even just a tiny bit. This is especially true given the tough time the share market has had recently, since nobody wants to go through another bear market.

I can't stress enough that you need to ignore all the chatter and noise that you hear about stocks on the news. The only things you need to be looking at are what you specifically hold and what the companies that you have invested in are doing financially. It really makes no difference whatsoever what everything else in the market is doing. If your stocks are doing well, then that should be enough. Warren Buffett once said that you should "only buy something that you'd be perfectly happy to hold if the market shut down for 10 years". And while I do tend to check back into my stocks once a year to make sure everything is still on track, all other times I try and ignore what is happening.

But What Happens If You Do Only Check Once A Year And You Find That The Companies Latest Reporting Is Less Than Stellar?

The only time you should consider whether to sell your investments is if the company's fundamentals have changed and they no longer represent a strong solid company. That means you need to go through the rules again with your company to see if it still fits them all. Is the ROE still above 15%? Has it taken on a lot of debt recently? Or, have its earnings growth turned negative?

Ignore what the current stock price is – the current price usually has nothing to do with whether the company is a great investment or not, and when the market is in good shape (as it will be again) then the price will eventually catch up.

If it still fits the rules, then I would recommend that you continue to hold on. Most of the time, you'll see that your investments will still fit all the rules and you don't need to sell. It's usually only in extreme cases that a good company gets itself into trouble. It was those investors that jumped ship when the share prices fell that got hurt the worst during the GFC. Those that held onto their investments are now in a much better position because the prices have rebounded and should continue to rise over the next few years.

But what about selling if the company has increased in price and you want to take a profit?

You're rich! The company you invested in has nearly doubled in price and you want to take your money and run. But should you?

Generally no (you'll kick yourself if it then goes on to triple in price and you missed out) but there are times when perhaps it's smart to go ahead and cash in. You'll need a pretty good reason to do so though. Just wanting to buy the latest iPad is not enough of a good reason (*I'm not saying it's not a good reason – I love my iPad – just that it's not a good enough reason to consider selling your investment*), but if you need the money because you have to pay off some debts then perhaps you might consider it.

When I was still new to stock investing and trying out different techniques there was many times when I thought I was so clever for taking a profit. I remember clearly one time that I bought into a company because a financial journalist of a newspaper I was reading predicted that this particular stock was about to rise and investors could double their money. I was sold and couldn't get my money into that company fast enough. And sure enough the price rose which caused me to do a little happy dance and once I had made what I thought was a good profit I sold it. This stock market game is easy I thought, until I checked and the price kept rising. "Oh no – I've got to get back into this." So I bought back in and for the first month or so everything went rosy, but the following month the stock price tanked and I panicked. I ended up selling at a loss. I was miserable and of course blamed the financial journalist for tricking me into investing into a stupid company.

A month later I checked and the price had bounced back, and over the next twelve months, even though it jumped around a lot, the stock price did rise. In fact had I continued to hold it, I would have made a very good profit. The journalist had made a good prediction based on sound company fundamentals, but I didn't know that at the time. It's only now in hindsight that I can thank him for his expensive lesson.

What About If Has Decreased In Price – Should You Sell Then?

Again I'd continue to hold if the fundamentals are still sound. As I've just mentioned those investors who continued to hold their stocks over the global financial crisis actually did better in the market than those who panic sold.

History tells us that over the long term the stock market will return around 10% p.a. That includes both good and bad years. The following chart shows the Dow Jones stock price over its history.

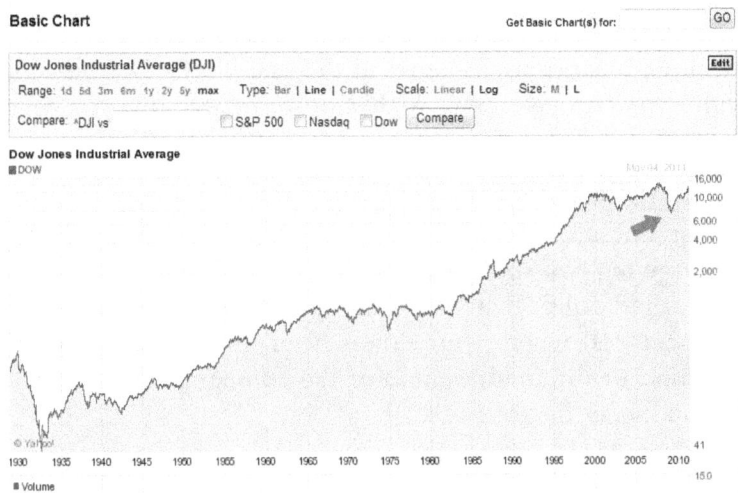

Figure 9.1 – *Dow Jones Industrial Average History from 1930 to present. Image screenshot from finance.yahoo.com*

See that little dip at 2008/2009 that I've pointed to with the arrow? That was our most recent market crash (GFC). It doesn't look quite as scary as it once did now that you can see it in context does it. In fact, right now the market is just about at the same highs that it was before the fall – so if you've held on tight with a bare knuckle grip while they plunged, by now you are probably doing ok – or at least breaking even. It's unclear at this stage whether the stock market will turn around with a strong uptrend or continue its volatility for another year or more. But if you can hold for the long term then history says that the price will increase again. You just need to wait it out and have faith.

So If I Shouldn't Sell If The Price Goes Up Or If The Price Goes Down, When Do I Sell?

If you are confused right now about when the right time to sell is, then you are not alone. In fact when it comes to selling your stocks, trying to figure out the best time is probably more difficult than choosing the stock in the first place. Or at least it is with long term investing. With short term investing you have your sell prices determined as soon as you buy, but long term is more of a 'wait and see' policy.

But that doesn't mean I'm going to leave you high and dry without giving you some guidance on the right time to sell. So far I've indicated that the only good time to sell your investments is when you either need the money for an emergency, or the fundamentals of the company have changed and it no longer fits the rules.

And while most of the time, they are the only two times that I recommend that you sell out of your investments, the reasons for investing in stocks in the first place should also be taken into consideration.

The most common reason that people want to invest in the stock market is because they see it as a way to build wealth. Of course there are many other reasons that people invest, from liking the company (perhaps you work for them), wanting to boast to your friends that you hold a piece of Disney, or even for the perks (some companies give discounts on their products to stockholders).

But let's assume that generally you bought because you wanted to make money. So it stands to reason then that if the company is now showing a good price you would rather have that income in your bank account where you can access it, than having a paper profit. But by selling out you'll also be missing out on dividends, future price increases, not to mention that you probably won't earn anything on your money in a regular bank account.

If you are retiring within the next five years then go ahead and cash out most or all of your investments and put the money into a high interest savings account (if you can find one). The hardest hit casualties of any stock market crash are those people who are relying on their stock market investments to fund their retirement.

If you are not retiring within the next five years then you need to look at whether your financial goals have been met or not. Perhaps you were saving up for a deposit on your first home and you've now reached that with a combination of savings and investment income – then by meeting that financial goal you should consider selling up so that you can realise your dream.

Having a clear goal about why you are investing in the first place can help determine whether selling up is the right choice for you. I sold a big portion of my portfolio when my partner and I purchased our first home together and for me that was the right decision. But if you haven't yet met your goals but want to sell out anyway because holding stocks is turning your hair grey every time you see a ticker showing how many points up or down the Dow has moved then either you need to sell your television or sell your shares so that you can find inner calm again. You can always get back into the market when you are feeling braver.

But for everyone else there is no need to sell up prematurely. Just forget about them and go on with your life. Pretty soon in a few years you can rejoice when you check back in at how much money you've made.

Conclusion – Where To From Here?

Well we've come to the end of my book 5 Simple Rules for Investing in the Stock Market. I hope that you've now been inspired to try out the rules with your own money, or at least test the waters first if you are still a bit nervous.

Having a good strategy in place is definitely the key to becoming successful investing in stocks. As you can see from my simple rules, every one of them is based on choosing companies with sound fundamentals and a good stable history of return for investors. And while past performance isn't a guarantee of future performance, you can at least have confidence that the companies that you are choosing to invest in have a good strong foundation and therefore have a much better chance of making money for you than choosing random stocks based on unfounded theories. These rules are the exact formula that I use every day to choose great companies to invest in - companies that have gone on to become very profitable for. I sincerely hope that you become successful in the stock market as well.

So the next step is to start researching. Get out there and see which companies fit the five rules and consider investing in them yourself. Or combine some of my rules with your own experiences so that you can come up with your own incredibly effective strategies.

What I like to do is take all the emotion out of it and just look at the numbers. I usually make a spreadsheet that contains all the five criteria as well as the EPS figure and the current price to make sure that it is trading at less than 16 x EPS. Each column on my spreadsheet relates to one of the rules and I highlight those companies that pass. That way I can see at a glance which companies fit all the criteria and I don't have to think about it too much. They either fit or they don't. And that's how I find stocks to invest in.

I've already got you started by showing you some great stocks within the Dow Jones (although company reporting time should be here again soon – which means you'll probably need to go through them again to make sure the figures are still similar) but it should get you started. I also plan on trying to add more strategies and tools on my blog in the future to help your investing further.

I hope you have found my book useful and you.

Good luck and I wish you a rich future!

Tracey

Want More?

Visit **http://www.simplerulesbooks.com** for more advice and articles about investing in the stock market, as well as other general finance advice.

About The Author

I am a writer and author. Having an entrepreneurial spirit my goal was always to make a full time living from my own pursuits without a boss. As I was always interested in finance and my dream was to become a successful writer it seemed inevitable I would combine the two and write about personal finance topics. I started investing in the stock market over ten years ago (in both Australia and overseas) as a way to become financially independent as I built up my writing career. I grew up in country Victoria (Australia) and now live in the bustling city of Sydney (still Australia).

My first book *Shopping for Shares: The Everyday Woman's Guide for Investing in the Australian Stock Market*, published by Wrightbooks became a bestseller in Australia. I followed that up a general finance title, *$0 to Rich: The Everyday Woman's Guide to Getting Wealthy* which was a guide that helped woman start from zero cash and build up to become rich by saving, investing and securing their money. Sort of like having your own financial coach on your bedside – except it was a book of course (I'm not sure many financial coach's like sitting on people's bedsides – but I could be wrong about that).

Tracey's Other Books

30 Day Spending Detox: The Simple Plan To Save Money and Get Out Of Debt in Just One Month

October 2011. Could you go thirty days without spending any money (except for the absolute essentials or course?). Author Tracey Edwards did just that and teaches you how to survive your own 30 Day Spending Detox and save a whole lot of money in the process to help you get out of debt or save for something special in just one month.

Shopping for Shares: The Everyday Woman's Guide to the Australian Stock Market

ISBN: 978-0-7303-7504-3 (2ND EDITION)

September 2011. Shopping for Shares is the essential girls guide to get you choosing, buying and profiting from the Australian stockmarket. Author, Tracey Edwards shares the strategies that have allowed her to leave her full-time job and support herself financially from her investments. Starting with only a small amount of money and gradually building it over time, these principles can be used by anyone, easily and successfully.

$0 to Rich: The Everyday Woman's Guide to Getting Wealthy

ISBN: 978-0-7314-0733-0

January 2008. Written specifically for women, $0 to Rich aims to be a girl's personal financial coach, guiding readers towards achieving their own financial goals by following five easy steps. Readers will learn how to define what 'rich' means to them and articulate exactly what they want. The book then explains how to set and achieve these financial goals over a defined time period.

Index

Return on Equity, 3, 7, 22, 23, 33, 34, 35, 36

S&P 500, 13, 23, 24, 31, 64, 68

Short Term Investing, 14, 15, 19, 55, 82

Stock Market Brokers, 17

T - AT&T, 30, 43, 64

TRV - The Travelers Company, 30, 55, 57, 58

UTX - United Technologies, 31, 60, 64

VZ - Verizon, 31

Warren Buffett, 13, 21, 33, 45, 53, 63, 71, 77, 78

WMT - Wal-Mart, 31, 60

XOM - Exxon Mobil, 31, 34, 60, 64

www.ingramcontent.com/pod-product-compliance
Lightning Source LLC
Chambersburg PA
CBHW071242170526
45165CB00003B/1203